What others say about this book:

To me, Kathy and Allan are very special people which made Legacy Pharmacy a very special place. Attention to their clients has always been above and beyond as is the expertise, knowledge and compassion they shared with one and all, in the world of alternative medicine. I am forever grateful for their friendship as well as their help through a difficult health issue and for also guiding me in ways to stay healthy naturally! Many thanks!
TP

I loved working at Legacy Specialty Pharmacy. Kathy went above and beyond to research what her customers needed. Allan would drop everything to go make a delivery so that the customers could have their compounded medicine as soon as possible. Kathy would research different ways for natural healing and often invited guest to come teach her as well as her customers about plants and natural healing. Kathy did not put time limits on her customers. Her number one priority was to be an advocate for them and help them achieve better health. The business truly was her and her husband's labor of love.
DF

Kathy was amazing how she could remember so much of what she had learned. Not only could she remember all the natural ways of helping people heal, but she could also retain all the intricate details of each of her customer's pain points. She's like an encyclopedia of knowledge wrapped in a warm and caring smile!!!
DI

Do No Harm

A Pharmacist's Journey

Kathy Hurst

An Intellect Publishing Book
Copyright 2024 Kathy Hurst

First Edition: 2024

ISBN: 978-1-961485-46-4 Hardback
ISBN: 978-1-961485-45-7 Paperback

FV-6

Contact the Author:
www.AuthorKathyHurst.com

Intellect Publishing, LLC
6581 County Road 32, Suite 1195
Point Clear, AL 36564

www.IntellectPublishing.com

Table of Contents

Appreciation

During the eight years our shop was open, we learned so much about the real truth about healthcare in America. We learned the reality of the good, bad and the ugly. Amidst our journey of discovery, we met some very memorable individuals. One man, a retired surgeon, is at the top of the list. From the first day I met him, he lit a flame of desire in me, a thirst for knowledge and truth. Wisdom and truth will set you free!!

I talk with him almost every day, even now. He is brilliant. He asks all the right questions, Why? When? How? Hemlock??? I want to thank him for his friendship, his encouragement and especially his requests for me to research the possibilities of better health in uncommon places. The results of these searches have been remarkable.

Introduction

Hello, My name is Kathy Hurst. I'm happy to introduce myself as a pharmacist. I've been registered since 1976 at 21 years old.

I began my career in hospital and practiced in clinical and retail. However, my love was always compounding. I owned my own specialty compounding pharmacy for eight years. We prepared prescriptions from scratch. Some of our common products were Bio-identical Hormones, medical lollipops for pain and nausea, facial and pain creams, nausea creams and medications for pets.

My love for compounding came from my grandparents. They owned a restaurant for several years. Their property was used to grow fruits and vegetables for their business. I still own the property and have developed 511 Rains Gardens. It is a generational project that will be passed to our son and daughter. My grandmother was a fabulous cook, but my grandfather was the herbalist. Herbs that he didn't grow himself came from Tommy Bass a well-known herbalist located near us at the foothills of the Appalachian Mountains. My grandfather made healing salves, hair tonics, vinegars, herbal extracts, and wines. I can still remember the sights and aromas of that childhood kitchen.

After doing a lot of research for two remarkable retired local surgeons interested in holistic and alternative medicine, we added a special room and division to the pharmacy. We began to offer testing for hormones, adrenals, neurotransmitters among other testing. We also developed programs and workshops that addressed specific disease entities and preventative health issues.

During our pharmacy time, we met lots of people that had simply slipped through the cracks of traditional medicine. With our tools and expertise, we were able to help them to doctors and modalities to nourish them to better health. We worked with many local physicians to help their patients. They were always complimentary and appreciative of our help. Our mission was to enable people to be an active part of their health and recovery.

Because of requests from many people, I have decided to use my knowledge and experiences to address the needs of people again. Not as a pharmacist but as a lifetime learner of many ways our bodies can heal and be healthy. I'm in the process of publishing several books and writing health notes on books we introduce on our podcast.

Come with me on this journey of helping YOU live a life of looking good, feeling good and staying healthy.

Do No Harm

A Pharmacist's Journey

Run and Not Grow Weary

Those who hope in the Lord will renew their strength.
They will soar on the wing like eagles:
they will run and not grow weary
they will walk and not be faint.
Isaiah 40:31•

I met a young man several years ago with a severe case of fibromyalgia. Helping him changed the course of my life. Today you would never know that he had ever been on the edge of going on disability. He was in constant pain, even to touch his skin was painful. His back muscles were drawing and knots formed throughout his body. His posture went from normal to distorted.

By the time we met, he had been to many doctors

including a rheumatologist, his primary care and chiropractors. Nothing seemed to help him. He finally was referred to a specialist that ran more specific tests than had been run previously. This specialist found a deficiency in hormones, amino acids and neurotransmitters. I was sent his prescription by the specialist.

When he came to pick up the medication, he explained his situation to me and asked for my help. That day, we formed a wonderful friendship. I began to research and found amazing ways to help people that mainstream medicine does not even consider. It took one man and almost forty years of working in the medical field to begin my journey of helping people get to the bottom of what is happening to their health and how to get their life back.

Mainstream medicine works within a tight framework of only maintaining a person's symptoms and never getting to the bottom of how to fix the problem. If my dear friend had not asked for help and wanted to help himself, I do not know where he would be today. I do not claim to know all the answers, but I am trained medically to do research and help people on their journey to recovery.

Angels Among Us

He shall give his angels charge over thee, to keep thee in all thy ways.
Psalm 91:11

Several years ago, a delightful country music legion, the group Alabama, recorded the song "Angels Among Us". Angels among us sent down to us from somewhere up above. They come in our darkest hour to show us the light of love.

Pray Believing. Believe that you can make a difference in this world, that you matter, that things seem grim but they will be better. Wake each morning Believing. You have a choice each day to be happy. Believe. Don't stop believing that your life can be all you dreamed for it to be.

Several years ago, a lady and her husband came to my shop. She was extremely overweight, was on 12 medications and her husband was very worried about her. No doctor had been able to help, so they sent her to the mental health center. She was told she was on too much medication and they tried to detox her. At that point, she had a seizure. She prayed that if she lived she would do whatever it took to be healthy. Her husband had watched a program on Public television and asked if I thought the book he purchased would help her.

I purchased my own book and read from cover to cover overnight. I recommended she follow the book and that I felt it would help her. I worked with her with diet, supplements, motivation and to our surprise she went from twelve medications to three and lost fifty pounds.

She brought me a before and after picture. She said she does not know the lady in the before picture because it is too painful. I saw a picture recently of artwork on quilts she was creating - it was beautiful

She believed she could get better and the Lord made a way. If her husband had not watched that program on Public television sent to him by angels and had not asked for help. Where would they be today?

Think Different

Whereas ye know not what shall be on the morrow. For what is your life? It is even a vapor that appears for a little time and then vanishes away.
James 4:14

We want to make this a year of positive change. In order to make a change you must THINK DIFFERENT. Everyone from 16 to 96 desires the same things.

Look Good

Feel Good

Smell Good.

In the weeks and months ahead, we will introduce

you to new natural innovative ways to stay young in body, mind and spirit.

First K.I.S.S

K (Keep)

I (It)

S (Simple)(Simple)

Making positive changes in our life does not have to be hard or require expensive products. Simple changes can make a dramatic difference in your life. Devote some time to simple positive change. We are only here for a llittle time. What we do with that time is entirely up to us. We are a vapor that then vanishes. Let this be the year to learn all you can about really living in the moments we have and being grateful for our blessings. Commit to THINK DIFFERENT. Make a difference in your life and the lives of others.

To Everything There is a Reason

To every thing there is a season, and a time to every purpose under the heaven. .A time to be born, and a time to die; a time to plant, a time to reap which is planted.
Ecclesiastes 3:1-8

To everything turn! turn! turn! there is a season turn! turn! turn! and a time for every person under heaven

(Turn! Turn! Turn! 1965 The Byrds)

The song is notable for being one of a few instances in popular music in which a large portion of scripture is set to music.

Look deeply into the picture above and imagine you are at the edge of the river. Can you see your reflection? What do you see? If what you see is not what you want to see shining back. Then this is the year to begin a positive change. Look deep within yourself and dig in your heels as you are about to embark on a journey of change.

THINK DIFFERENT.

Keep open to possibilities and let your inner spirit guide you. "Let nature be thy medicine." There is a season for everything. This is YOUR season to become everything you were meant to be. You were not put on this earth to be lethargic, unhappy, full of pain, overweight and helpless. You are here for a PURPOSE. So, now do your part and THINK DIFFERENT.

Epigenetics tells us that just because our mother, grandmother and every other relative in our family has diabetes that we are destined to suffer. NO, YOU can make a choice what goes into your mouth.

Think reducing Blood Sugar Levels Without Drugs is Impossible? Take the 30-Day Skeptic's Challenge "Health Science Journal" Complimentary January 2016 Issue

Do not blame grandmother for your choices because there are personal lifestyle choices behind deadly diabetes.

A lifestyle of bad eating habits that include foods loaded with wheat, sugar and high fructose corn syrup.

A lifestyle of sedentary living eating processed foods on the couch instead of exercising.

To eliminate blood sugar problems, all you need to do is eat natural foods and lots of protein. Avoid wheat (Bread, cakes, pastries) and sugar. And get your muscles activated. To prove this works, take this simple challenge.

First, start with an accurate glucose meter to take daily readings (as you should always do.)

Next, stop eating sugar, wheat and any foods containing them. When in doubt READ THE LABEL.

And finally, start exercising your muscles.

Compare your glucose readings from Day 1 to Day 30. You'll be absolutely amazed at your results. But you probably need some help in getting those numbers where they should be. Looking forward to sharing tips on how to detox from sugar. If you take the 30-day challenge and see improvements in your blood sugar levels then you are ready for another look at your reflection in the river. Then, you my friend are ready for a plunge in the river.

Get ready to LOOK GOOD and FEEL GOOD! :

Spread the News
Eat Fat, Get Thin

Make a joyful noise unto the Lord, all ye lands. Serve the Lord with gladness, come before his presence with singing.
Psalm 100 :1-2•

Watching closely what I eat became much more important to me today. Several years ago, my husband and I mastered the art of cutting sugar from our diet. At the time, our greatest love was sweet tea. Each week we met with a client that was trying to lose weight and get healthier. On a regular basis, she began to ask if we were still drinking sweet tea. I knew if we did not walk the walk, we could not talk the talk. So, we conquered the sugar and artificial sweetener demons,

Today, I read shocking news about fat that solidified what a good friend had been telling me for over a year. Fat is not our enemy. We have been told for years to eat less fat, so we started eating more pasta, muffins and carbs. My friend eats more fat less carbs and has lost weight that she has been able to keep off. She looks good and feels good.

People are continuing to ask for her secret.

It is remarkable how changes to our diet can make such improvements to our overall health.

Hippocrates was right when he said, "Let food be thy medicine".

One of my favorite author's Dr. Mark Hyman has published a new book Eat Fat Get Thin. He is a functional medicine doctor which means he gets to the bottom of why we get fat and sick. Several of our clients have seen Dr. Hyman as patients with wonderful results.

Seven Tips to Natural

Just what is Natural? Sunshine on your face. The taste of fresh picked strawberries. A meadow of spring flowers or maybe lavender. The smell of rain. A walk on the beach. A sleigh ride in fresh fallen snow.

The list is enless. What Natural is, is what Keeps us Healthy.

Go back to the basics and really live again. Simplify everything. Get in tune with nature.

Walk barefoot in the morning when the dew is still on the grass or on pure beach sand. "Earthing" Relax and let your inner compass guide you to peace and tranquility. Read a book, do yoga, listen to music, meditate, dream, appreciate and use nature's apothecary.

Give me seven tips to Natural

(1) Beware of the company that proclaims to be natural and has 10 unknown ingredients in their natural products.

(2) Read and understand the 12 endocrine disruptors from EWG

EWG (Environmental Working Group)

(3) Make your own healthcare products (DIY) so your understand what each ingredient does and the reason it is free from dangerous chemicals.

(4) Grow your own garden if possible. Look for the benefits of eating foods the color of the rainbow.

(5) Eat grass feed meats only if at all. The story about antibiotic use in grain feed cattle is revolting.

(6) What and how we cook is one of the easiest ways to prevent almost all disease.

(7) Our six best doctors-sunshine, water, rest, air, exercise and diet

Red Cadillac

Many people with different health issues appeared at the door of our little shop. However, this one was quite unique. This lady had been told the dreaded words, You Have Cancer. At that time, we were extremely tiny, sandwiched between an accountant on one side and a beauty shop on the other side. The male beautician had become our greatest fan. He already had a wonderful loyal following and after his client's appointments he would send them to our shop to get acquainted and learn about what we offered in natural products.

One day one of those ladies appeared at our door with very bad news. Her doctor had rudely given her the death sentence that she had lung cancer and if she did not have chemo immediately, she would die.

At that moment she did not like that doctor, she was scared and wanted to know all alternative things we could tell her or offer her.

I began researching things to build her immune system, nutrition, supplements, everything. I also suggested removing her estrogen patch might be a good idea. I found her another local doctor that gave her a second opinion. She was financially able to afford most any type of treatment. I reached out to other facilities for information for her. She was happy and encouraged about all of the information. A few days passed and she walked in to say she had reviewed all the information we had provided her and had made a decision. She was going to have chemo with the original oncologist. The doctor she had said was rude. The chemo she had not wanted to do.

Had she lost it? What was her reasoning? Had she given herself ample time to make such a decision about her life? When a person is placed in a position like hers it takes courage, faith and grace to make a decision. No one, not your doctor, not your spouse, not your children, not your parents, not your friends and especially not me is entitled to make that decision. So I asked her, What can I do now to help you? If you want us to help you then your doctor must be willing to allow communication between us. The doctor will probably agree you are not ready mentally or physically today for chemo. How long does he consider is appropriate to get your immune system in shape? I can help you build your immune system. I wanted the oncologist to critique all nutrition and supplemental recommendations. We became part of her healthcare team.

She became very aware of the importance of watching what she ate. Supplements like sea vegetables and medicinal mushrooms were added with the oncologist blessings. She was prescribed topical nausea medicine that we prepared for her. More supplements were added from time to time and always with the oncologist knowledge.

Several patients with her same diagnosis were being

treated at the same time. None of those patients worked with unbiased nutritional, supplemental, emotional help. She survived they did not.

The day she was declared cancer free she drove up to our shop in a brand-new red Cadillac. It was a gift from her dear husband to her for surviving cancer. She took me for a drive to tell me how grateful she was for my help in her survival.

Eissac Tea

I was introduced to Eissac Tea in a most unexpected way. Our shop was new and we welcomed any way we might be of service helping people achieve wellness. Most days after the hairdresser closed his shop next door he would come by and explore new items we might have received that day. One of his favorites was the pajamas made of wicking that allowed women to enjoy a cool comfortable night's sleep. He named them hot flash pajamas and recommended them to his clients for us. We appreciated his enthusiasm and the enormous help he provided our new growing business.

He was also a spokesperson and platform artist for a natural haircare company. He went all over the United States and several countries promoting his line of hair products. The products were so good even the local oncologist sent him patients that were having problems with their hair. Since he also had a chemistry background, he understood and was able to explain why these natural hair products worked so well. We were pleased to have him speak many times at healthcare events that we held at the shop.

So, one day he dropped by the shop to tell me he had ordered four herbs. He had gotten a bad diagnosis from his doctor, had done his own research and wanted my opinion on his findings. I researched myself and found the four herbs make up essiac tea. I felt it was fabulous. He had hit the jackpot. The name eissac came from the Canadian nurse that developed the recipe. It is her name Cassie spelled backwards. E-I-S-S-A-C

I found later that several reputable companies make Eissac tea. But, at that time the chemist developed his own plan and eradicated his health issue and stunned his doctor.

My love of this type concept began from humble begins in my grandparents kitchen filled with herbs and spices. It is amazing how opening my mind to possibilities and allowing people to ask my opinion helped broaden my view and perspective on healthcare.

We were open at night to accommodate people who worked 8 to 5.

Those hours allowed visitors to come and discuss other natural remedies and concoctions like Essiac Tea that they were familiar with. This was an awakening of a new type of pharmacist within me. A pharmacist that was willing to blend old and new ways of helping people heal. Not the pharmacist that was held hostage to only modern medicine. But, the pharmacist that from that moment forward was open to the fact that old remedies could still work and just might be what the person really needed.

The Scan

I tried to make each person that walked into the door of our shop feel special. For me it is important for a person to know someone cares. This type of empathy plays a big part in their recovery. Even though schools try to teach this, to me you are either born with the capacity to want to help others or not.

Each person is different, and their treatment plan should be individualized. If they know and understand about their health issues, they can be a vital part of their own healing. They are the one residing in the reality of their own health issue. They can tell you how it feels, what has helped, what hasn't or rudimentary techniques they have acquired to adapt. After the picture has been exposed the next step is to put the puzzle pieces together and search for a solution. Listening and then searching through your mind's archives is an excellent method. Or, it has served me well. I began being the conscious observer.

One day a lady came by in a major panic. She had just had a mammogram and was informed that she was scheduled for another one due to unexplained findings. She did not want to wait. Her heart was racing. Her mind was leading her to dark places. The unknown had taken on a scary scenario for her. At that point, as a healthcare professional you have to pull from everything you have read, seen, heard, anything that will calm and make sense.

I had recently attended a workshop about women's health. The workshop had extended longer than expected. Some of the speakers talked in a monotone and were just boring. When I left I felt the whole event just did not live up to what I had expected. But, one of the presentations was about a unique type of scan

All I had to say was thermography. I had to spell it for her t-h-e-r-m-o-g-r-a-p-h-y. I did not know who provided the service, the cost, nothing. All I knew was the presentation had been interesting enough for me to remember and had sounded like a well-researched type of scan. Something I would have pursued myself if needed.

Several days went by and I received a phone call, the lady had researched thermography on her own. She had found a local place that provided the service and had it done. One word had made an entire difference in the outcome. Her scan turned out well and she was relieved.

The scary part of heath care is the unknown. To me, it is the new age of keeping people in the dark. If people do not know or understand they can be controlled. For some people it is easier and they just do not care. For others, finding the method to better health is a goal that can be achieved. For this lady she became empowered. One word and her desire to find an answer. I wanted then and still do encourage people to stay healthy through proactive behavior. You are the master of your own destiny and health legacy.

Good Vibes

We tried to make a ritual of having workshops and presentations on a regular basis. I was blessed to have meet such a passionate holistic nutritionist. She had a wonderful way of captivating an audience. Her many programs at the shop included themes we promoted in our business, such as Sugar Busters, Detox Your House and Longevity.

She and I shared a thirst for all types of modalities that can help a person recover from bad health and heal. She is a veteran and understands exactly the traumas that war can place on an individual. After she returned to the states, she was not sure how to handle what life had thrown her way. At first, she allowed the professionals to try their luck at helping her. She then chose to take holistic classes and became her own patient advocate. She is educated in how nutrition and supplements play such an important role in people's health.

She was even asked by the local Heart Association to do a presentation for them. She is one of those people that can explain every aspect of a health problem and understands how to develop ways to help that standard of care never even considers. "Let food be thy medicine." She and I both are educated to know the difference between healthcare and sickcare.

People should not be encouraged to continue bad health behavior because someone can benefit financially from that bad behavior.

Nowadays, if they can give a medical situation a name then they can give a drug for it. Many of these situations when I was young were addressed or considered acceptable. For example, why has it become acceptable by American society to lower someone's immunity to disease in order to maybe have clearer skin? When you lower someone's immunity you destroy their body's ability to fight any disease. Think Cancer.

She and I both are strongly concerned with back to basics healthcare. We call it "Good Vibes". It is a common thread of introducing people to researched methods that they may not be aware. Open your eyes, your ears and mind to hope and possibilities of better health.

Relaxed Conversation

Sometimes a relaxed atmosphere and casual conversation is all it takes to solve a daunting health issue.

A lady appeared at the shop one day with a request for information about a serious sinus problem she was having. Her ENT had told her that sinus surgery might be her only option. She had several rounds of antibiotics and steroids and her condition had continued to deteriorate. I took her information and asked her to return in a couple of days to acquire more information from her that might help.

After several meetings with her, she began to relax and share just routine conversation. How are you feeling today? Has anything about your health condition changed? How about your life in general?

Questions doctors don't ask and definitely don't have time to ask. I call it relaxed conversation. So, that day in the quiet of the moment the lady says, I purchased a new GE refrigerator several months ago. I replied that's nice. Typical relaxed conversation that allowed her to be at ease. It was her following statement that resonated volumes. Her statement was, And I think it has mold. Mold??? Did you say mold? In the deep south where we have 90 to 100 degree summers and the breeding ground for everything she thinks she has MOLD. She had called the local dealer where she purchased the refrigerator and asked for a repairman to check her appliance. He had found nothing wrong.

She wanted a replacement but the dealer was not going to replace it.

I told her we needed to investigate this ourselves. I did some research and found a company in Atlanta that sold petri dishes that she could place in the refrigerator and around her kitchen and other rooms to verify mold. She placed the petri dishes in the suggested locations and gave adequate time. We sent them back for clarification and sure enough we received pictures and identification that mold was growing. After viewing the information she provided, GE replaced her refrigerator. There was a defect in the ice making apparatus and it was causing the mold growth. The same company that supplied the petri dishes also supplied cleaning supplies and instructions about the process with a local company to continue with the eradication of the mold. She followed the procedures and her mold problem disappeared and so did her sinus issue. Her ENT informed her she would not have to have sinus surgery now.

A casual conversation and a little detective work solved a health issue that could have only gotten worse. Making time to listen to people is an important part of what is missing in our healthcare system today.

I learned that I was the conduit to situations. We

helped many, many people in our tiny shop. By listening to people and researching I could grasp concepts that went unnoticed. A way to solve health issues based only on a medical background and the drive to do the research needed to guide people to a solution. I did not diagnose, treat or cure I was simply the observer and bridge that got them to the place they needed to be.

Herbs and Spices

When we enlarged the consulting, gathering area we had room for several filing cabinets. Anytime our customers or I found interesting material it was labeled put in a folder and filed. The researched information was utilized daily. We were lucky to find a lovely, retired nurse that volunteered to file and expand the research area. She was well educated in herbs and holistic medicine. She had worked in several states in doctor's offices and clinics. She was in her element amongst the books and research materials. She had her own system of filing and kept us aware of new and interesting developments.

Her enthusiasm was contagious. She was a talented cook and brought dishes containing items we had never tried before. One day she surprised us with a dish containing quinoa. Allan and I both thought it looked like bird seed but it was delicious. We were learning new ways to eat and being introduced to books like "Forks over Knives: The meals she was preparing from herbs and spices were luscious. She loved Dr. Mark Hyman's book "Blood Sugar Solutions" and the recipes. One of our customers had benefited greatly from his book and recipes.

I got a call from Allan that our volunteer had called

him and said she was visiting her daughter in Pennsylvania. She also said she was at the doctor's office- Dr. Hyman's office. I could not believe she was really seeing the author and noted speaker -the real Dr. Mark Hyman. She shared her testing results and treatment plans. We both learned valuable information and were introduced to products we did not know even existed. We were excited about placing the order and receiving the new items. Dr. Hyman used natural ways of handling things instead of adding more scripts that would just treat symptoms.

Later that year she moved to live with her children. We understood that because of her age she needed to be close to family. We missed her and think of her often.

Unfaltering Faith

My personal assistant became a lifelong friend. Her views on life, spirituality and health are remarkable. By profession she is a schoolteacher but is much more than that. Her computer skills were phenomenal. She developed an entire website of natural products including pictures and product descriptions for the shop. She also held workshops about essential oils. When I was unable to attend local events she would go in my place and take notes. A most memorable event was a presentation on Israel of which we were both interested.

Israel has some of the best cancer centers in the world.

We worked together as a team. She could finish my own sentences.

She was an awesome personal assistant and kept the shop running in tip top shape. She was so friendly and good with people. Customers adored her.

She is a lifelong learner and attributes her genuine qualities to her unfaltering faith. She is the mother of three lovely children that are never sick. She has taught them from infancy techniques to keep them healthy. Her faith keeps her busy with mission trips all over the world. Costa Rica is her favorite. I was so disappointed to lose her when she had to relocate with her husband. He took a position as a youth pastor at another church in another state.

No, Not Today

During the time our shop was open we helped several people that had one time been placed in a mental healthcare facility. The sad truth was all their stories were the same. They had been treated with standard of care by several different doctors. If they did not respond or get better they were told they were the reason they were not getting better.

The healthcare professional's reasoning was repulsive. They blamed the patient. They were told they were not taking their meds, they were not taking them correctly or their own systems were not responding properly. Never were these patients told there were other ways to handle their medical situation. Most of the time they were placed in the mental facility after the patient was exhausted from trying everything those doctors had wanted them to do. They had finally had enough and were combative and said, "No More, I am done." These people were intuitive enough to want to live and willing to search for other possibilities.

These situations are sad to me, because we live in a civilized country that should be willing to treat each person on their terms and guided to what really works no matter how simply or complex the treatment. It would be nice to get back to the basics of healthcare and get to the root cause of the problem first. We should begin with a simpler approach unless the issue is critical that day. Explain the issue and give simple adjustments to diet, exercise and lifestyle that the patient can try first before any medications are added. It would give the patient ample time to try to reclaim their health. If the issue took years to appear then today is not the day to hit it with a sledgehammer.

Many of our people were considered mental simply because their gut feeling said "No Not Today" and they saved their own lives.

One lady was on many medications and several doctors. Some of her medications were for pain, some for anxiety, some for depression. Not one doctor had sat with her like another human being and said, How can I help you? Instead they wrote more and more scripts. The doctor was happy, the pharmaceutical companies were happy, the pharmacy was happy and everyone that got paychecks from that maze of sickcare. But, that day in the cold office someone said NO.

Instead of dealing with the mess, she was sent to even greater maze for people that society writes off. Some people in mental healthcare do have serious problems. But, we would probably be amazed to find out lots of these people just function on a different level. A functioning level that if addressed properly could really be helpful to society.

Instead they are sent there to be medicated to a point of being totally controlled. These are truths observed from several people who even survived the maze for up to twenty years and lived to finally be able to live free among us.

Nursing homes are popular for medicating people to the point of total control, especially at night. They can get by with not hiring more people to help with their patients. Society allows them to medicate someone's mother, grandmother, aunt, uncle, so no one has to be bothered with them.

Each time we dealt with a person that had previously been placed in a mental health facility were extremely willing to help themselves be heathier. So, if you are a friend or family member of someone that is on lots of medications and does not seem to be getting better or even worse. Please be a patient advocate and guide that person to someone that can help them. You and your loved one will be so glad you did.

Nadine Johnson- The Herb Lady

I met Ms. Nadine at a meeting of like-minded people arranged by one of our customers. From the beginning, I felt I had known her my whole life. She was lively, cheerful and a wonderful storyteller. She reminded me of friends of my grandparents. She was and still is an encyclopedia on herbs and old remedies.

She had even owned her own herb shop and garden. She was also a nurse and worked for a female physician which was very unusual for the deep south years ago. The way that doctor practiced was very much like naturopathic doctors. She got to the root cause of medical issues instead of just treating symptoms.

Ms. Nadine's later days of nursing were in the cardiac unit of a local hospital. She went into early retirement due to health issues. She researched the issue herself and developed a workable protocol. She was very familiar with old and new types of treatments. On many occasions I would call her for her view on certain health issues, especially if I felt an herbal suggestion would be appropriate.

She introduced me to the wonderful world of herbs, again. As a child I had grown up seeing my kitchen filled with jars of vinegars, wines and fresh and dried fruits and herbs. My grandmother was the chief but my grandfather was the one fascinated with herbs. I can still remember the sights and aromas from that kitchen. It left a lasting impression in a little girl's mind of how health could be attained from nature.

We went on nature walks with Ms. Nadine and listened contently for hours about herbal treatments and how rural America handled medical issues years ago. We often attended local and state herbal events together. We enjoyed and appreciated the presentations she held at our shop. She is a prolific writer and wrote articles for the Farmer's Cooperative Magazine for years. She has published several books including a cookbook. I was honored to be asked to write a testimonial for her in her latest book- "Nadine Johnson-Ther Herb Lady"

Tea Time

Search through history and you will find emperors, tribesmen and even princess enjoying the benefits of tea. The medicinal qualities and uses are limitless.

When a dear friend and former co-worker started building her own business she included teas as one of the staples in her line of products. I had watched her enjoy all types of teas when we worked together years ago. We got first-hand experience in the new age mega pill mills. Lots of prescriptions w2nt through that pharmacy in the tune of 500 to 600 per day. Talk about stress and pressure, you had to be physically and mentally alert from the time you walked in to the time you left.

My son's track coach made the comment, He knew where our son got some of his running ability. We felt like we were running a championship track event every day we worked. This environment provided a great opportunity for my friend to determine if the teas really worked the way the literature presented them. Properties such as calming, endurance, focus and more could be analyzed. She learned a lot of value information to use in her line of teas.

She and I have remained close friends through the years. We have a common bond of enjoying teaching people new and innovative ways to stay healthy. We both opened our business at the same time. We opened a compounding pharmacy and she and her husband a physician developed an herbal line of specialty products. Her unique line of teas consists of teas for flu prevention, teas to build your immune system, teas for sleep, inflammation, and the list continues to expand. Each herbal item is grown and harvested on her coastal farm for guaranteed freshness and purity.

I admire her tenacity and patience. Opening a new line of herbal products is not an easy task. Fine tuning and developing each item is extremely difficult. But she and her husband have done a marvelous

job, and the products are amazing. Products in her line consist of shampoo, conditioners, soaps, facial masks and more. Also, herbal blends of curcumin, bamboo, nettle and moringa are included in her specialty herbal line.

We were fortunate to carry her lovely products in our store. She also held workshops. The shop always smelled so nice from the aromas of her teas, soaps and specialty products.

She has spent lots of time perfecting the texture, the smell and the delivery of each of her items. Her recipes come from herself, her husband and professional relatives that saved a legacy for generations to come. I want to applaud her and recommend her line of products to anyone that reads this book.

Dr. Nettles Natural Beauty

I Had A Dream

graduated from a small high school in a class of 107 students. Four of us shared our career dreams with each other and at the time it made perfect sense. Teresa B's dream was to be a doctor, Teresa D. was to be a nurse. I was to be a pharmacist and Deb was to be a mortician.

These were big dreams for four young girls from small town USA. Teresa D. and I became our dreams. The stars just did not align for Teresa B. and Deb. It is ironic how life can throw curve balls to our life dreams. Now, it seems hilarious to imagine Deb a mortician. Her humorous, outgoing personality would be odd in the framework of a funeral home.

Life sent her in other directions. The greatest gift to me was she became the godmother to our two children. Her wit, humor, grace, and outside the box way of looking at things helped shape our children into the gracious free spirits they are today. Thank you Deb, for being such a fundamental part of my life and the lives of our children.

My career aspirations really began for me in middle school. My friends told me I was the only person they knew that made their own toothpaste. A simple recipe I adapted from trial and error. The texture had to be appealing and so did the taste. It had to make my teeth feel clean and not leave a bitter after taste. I was not pleased with a medicine taste either. I suppose I did OK for an amateur because I have had no cavities.

Having my own little shop was a part of that dream from years before. A lab with mortars and beakers and scales and ingredients of powders and liquids was definitely in that dream. I had a dream and it became real.

Compounding is the essence of pharmacy but a dying art slowly being taken away. We worked really hard in our little shop to provide the best products and quality service but were no match to the powers that want small community compounding to not exist. It will be a sad day for healthcare if we allow greed, lies and deceit to destroy the very fabric of our healthcare system.

Val

She lived such a unique colorful life. Several years before, she had owned a lovely dress shop. She developed her own line of Mardi Gras gowns. One night after hours she came and showcased different types of gowns she had made and sold. The dresses were gorgeous. The fabrics were lovely and I admired her workmanship. She was truly a talented creator and seamstress. At one time I felt I had ruined a cute aqua pant suit with bleach. She took that pant suit added antique lace to the bleached areas and made the suit look like a new outfit. I was shocked and delighted at her creativity.

Val was also a nurse. That profession served her well when her mother became sick and bedridden.

We did our compounding at the shop at night for delivery the following day. However, we delivered Val's medicines after we closed late at night. Her mother got her days and nights mixed up so they slept during the day and were up all night.

Her delivery time was always a humorous one for conversation. We also delivered to the funeral home. An employee at the funeral home had an animal that got a monthly compound. So, we delivered to the funeral home once a month. It was not unusual to see Allan delivering to beauty shops, nail salons, restaurants, grocery stores. The delivery went anywhere the customer wanted it delivered. Val delighted in the fact that she was the only late-night delivery.

We planned an event with an iridologist. I could not be at the shop that day so I called my fill in pharmacist and Val. My pharmacist wanted to observe and I knew Val was knowledgeable with medical terminology. She would have to be the transcriptionist for the iridologist. She was happy to be able to participate even though it was a day event.

Val was able to keep her mother alive for many years simply because she was knowledgeable and such a good nurse. Allan and I learned so much from Val about love, life and the real importance of family when your health begins to fail you. She was definitely a unique caring individual.

R.I.P. Val

We love and miss you.

Triumph Over Adversity

When we moved to our new location we made the lab smaller and allowed more space for the consulting, gathering area. We added a couch and an educational area for more books. People would come in just to see books and products we had added to the new area.

The couch seemed to be the landing spot for regular customers. Even though the area had a 50's glider and two additional chairs the couch was the favorite seat. It must have made the area more inviting and comfortable.

A nice young man dropped by to ask if we could order some products for him. We were always excited to add interesting items to our growing inventory. As we became more acquainted with him we were astonished by his medical story. Eventually, we made a film of his story. It was true and real and amazing. He experienced a medical mishap where standard of care failed someone terribly. He is an excellent example of triumph over adversity. When the medical system let him down he knew in his heart there were other ways to better health. I am so thankful he shared his story with us. We learned so much from him about resilience and the will to leave a positive legacy for his family. It was a true story of faith, help from unfamiliar places and natural products.

Buddy

Our shop was filled with such interesting customers. When we first opened our son marketed the business for us and brought us prescriptions from an array of different modalities. He did an excellent job. He had learned in college and training from PCCA unique ways to approach medical professionals that utilize compounded prescriptions.

The local pet store had a veterinarian on staff and some of our first scripts were for animals. Some of the guinea pigs at the pet store had a fungus. This problem had caused their hair to come out in spots. This was not an appealing sight for buyers to see. For us, it was a golden opportunity to introduce her skills. The veterinarian called us, and we prepared an antifungal medication that the guinea, liked. Now, the pet store had sellable guineas.

Each set of animals were unique in their likes and dislikes. Cats seemed to be the most finicky in smell, taste and texture. If the cat did not like the product it would hiss and walk away. We finally perfected a cod liver oil tuna cocktail that was popular for them. We learned to interview the owners of any sick animal to find out what food, smells and tastes the animals liked. It was sometimes a challenge to please the animal but to see them healthy again was the reward.

A memorable animal was Buddy. He was a cute, feisty, doggie that was a ball of fur. The owners had moved to a new house that had an upstairs. Buddy was fascinated by the stairs. He would run up the stairs and down the stairs, over and over, until he strained some muscles. His owners tried unsuccessfully to give him what the vet offered. Finally, the exhausted vet called in a compound for an old muscle relaxer in a liquid form. The formula worked wonders for him but it took several refills to get enough in his system for him to be his active self again.

Buddy was so happy that he could distinguish Allan's truck making the delivery and came running like he knew his good medicine was being delivered. When winter came and their driveway was icy, Buddy experienced another bout of strained muscles. The owners had the vet call in another refill to us for Buddy. They said they knew how effective the previous script had been to Bubby's recovery.

Spacetabs

The clientele at our shop consisted of many healthcare professionals. We had doctors, nurses, dentist, physical therapist, massage therapist, pharmacist and the list goes on. One day one of those professionals brought in a prescription to compound a similar medication to what I had remembered from back in the 70's at the beginning of my career. I was elated to make such an interesting product.

I remembered seeing ads for that product in magazines. The ads showed several women in the waiting room of a doctor's office. All the women were dressed differently with different hair but all the faces were the same. The medication was so versatile it could be used for so many female problems. Remember the seven dwarfs of menopause, itchy, bitchy, bloated, sweaty, forgetful, sleepy, and all dried up. A good reason for the removal of the product has never been real clear to me.

The tablet was reflective of the historic 70's revolution. It was round and adorned with psychedelic yellows, green's, browns and looked a lot like a map of the earth with oceans and continents.

The ingredients were just as colorful. A combination

of the ingredients that created a treatment for female issues that did not contain any hormones. It was workable, appropriate and relative to how healthcare was addressed during that time period.

Even the trademark was unique. They were called Spacetabs. It was my idea of how earth looked from space.

Even one of the ingredients had a historical connotation. One theory surfaced that back in the 1600's a group of women were thought to have taken something close to one of the ingredients in extremely large doses and began to exhibit odd behavior. The behavior was so bizarre the locals thought they were witches and they were burned at the stake.(The Salem Witches).

Sad that hundreds of years later, it was found that tiny amounts of the ingredient in combination with a few other ingredients could actually help women with hormonal problems.

If one medication can address so many female issues and not disrupt or add to hormone levels, why would it not still be commercially available? A google search revealed more specific medications were developed. Really???

I even googled what company originally produced the product.

Luckily, I had saved the ad from the 70's and know exactly what company made the original product.

Protect the Girls

Unfortunately, people are highly influenced by programs like "Run for a Cure." Instead of introducing preventative educational healthcare, America sits back and waits until terrible things develop. Then the greed machine comes out in full force to rake in the profits from this health tactic.

At our shop, we chose to introduce people to preventative medicine with our presentations and workshops.

"Protect the Girls" was a well-planned event that included a holistic nutritionist, a hairdresser that worked with cancer patients, a lady that owned a thermography business and several women that had survived breast cancer.

I realized how important preventative strategies were when a customer's sister came for my help. She had survived breast cancer twice and was afraid if it happened again, she would not make it. That sparked the need for research on prevention.

I had read the book by Dr. Zava, "What your doctor does not tell you about breast cancer". That book alone transformed my business into one that specialized in women's health issues. The shop's first script was for a women's hormone cream.

Before we opened, I had vowed not to put a lot of effort into talking with women about hormones. Several years before, I had worked part time at a compounding pharmacy owned by a male pharmacist.

Thursday was my permanent day and he channeled all of the women's hormone questions to me. I must have talked to hundreds of itchy, bloated mad women. I felt exhausted by the fact that there was not a lot in compounding that could be done at that time except what I did to listen and sympathize. So, I vowed not to go through those struggles in a business of my own.

Shortly after we opened, I called Dr. Zava's lab about saliva testing for hormones. They told us to attend several of their workshops. We learned how to instruct women and men in the testing and how for us to be able to read the test results. This was such a wonderful refreshing progression for me from the days of only listening to hormone problems. Because of those workshops, hormone issues became an important part of our business. Now, when a person asked why a certain regiment was written by their doctor, we were able to explain.

We worked closely with the patients and their doctors. Once a doctor continued to increase a lady's testosterone in her compound. She called to tell us she was growing a mustache. Her doctor was notified, and he reduced her dosage. Being a patient advocate and close confidant allowed people to understand and be more confident with their protocols.

After our research on breast cancer prevention, we decided an event would be appropriate. I called ZRT lab and they sent lots of great suggestions and information. We modeled our event on their researched literature and strategies.

We began the event with 5 important questions:

(1) How does the patient handle stress? We know from other cancers that stress correlates with tumor development. Protocols for handling stress need to be addressed.

(2} How balanced is this patient's endocrine system? Various processes need to be checked, blood sugar, thyroid, hormones, sleep issues or even irregular menstrual cycles.

(3) Are they getting optimal nutrition? Levels need to be checked such as magnesium, iodine, selenium, B vitamins. Do they know and understand the importance of cruciferous vegetables?

(4} Is the liver operating properly to produce safe metabolic products? Are cancer promoting metabolites being formed?

(5} Is this patient eliminating properly? How many bowel movement per day? How about regular exercise and even sweating? Is the digestive tract sluggish?

People do not realize how the body works in harmony. It is like a symphony, if a part is not functioning properly it can cause other parts to be off tract.

We learned a lot from this hormone research and continued to share this at our shop.

Iridology

Life teaches us many ways to stay healthy. Some people are armed with more tools than others. Knowledge is power.

Learning new ideas rewires the brain to expand its capability to understand and grasp new concepts. To remain close minded blocks the realm of possibilities.

During our eight years in business, we were introduced and learned many interesting and scientifically proven health modalities that most people including ourselves were not aware even existed.

A talk with Ms. Nadine, the herb lady, opened our eyes literally to an exciting unique way to see what is happening in our body. She had through the years become friends with an iridologist. Ms. Nadine believed this lady years before had saved her husband's life. He had gotten sick with some very vague symptoms. Ms. Nadine took him to the iridologist that read his eyes and suggested the type doctor that could help him. After following her directions he was tested, treated and had a perfect recovery. The results could have turned out deadly if this kind professional had not been knowledgeable.

Throughout history the eyes have been considered

the mirror of the soul. The science of iridology can help indicate what may be going on in the body. The logic behind this is that thousands of nerves or energies run from every tissue and organ of the body, ending in the tips of your fingers and toes as well as the iris of your eyes.

The iridologist came to our shop twice to read eyes. Both visits were well received by locals and customers. She was booked solid every thirty minutes from 9 to 5 on both occasions. It was amazing to us how accurate and helpful she was to our turnout of people.

After hours she read our eyes and explained to us how the procedure was performed. A chart is used that resembles a clock and each part of the body is represented on the chart. Spots and characteristics within the eye reveal problems that are happening within the body.

We were blessed to be able to introduce people to old and new ways to keep people informed and educated about good health.

Use It or Lose It

Our mission with our workshops was to build a bridge for people to better health. We introduced simple useful programs that were researched and designed to provide lasting benefits.

Sometimes life can be totally overwhelming. I called it the Big 4. Grief, Anxiety, Depression and Stress (GAPS) take people in daunting directions. At our shop we addressed these life challenges with many programs and workshops on a small scale. But later we would realize how important tackling them on a larger basis would have been for others and ourselves. Thankfully we provided "Use It or Lose It" on a scale that produced positive action plans by lots of people.

Most everyone knows someone that now has or has passed away with Alzheimer's. The movie, "The Notebook" made this issue up front and personal. I really have watched the movie over and over again.

The beauty of the story to me was that Ally (the wife) wrote a book of their life before she was deeply affected for (her husband) Noah to read to her as the disease progressed. And she promised if she could she would return to him even if only in moments.

This concept was the premise of choosing this

wonderful protocol developed by Dr. Vincent Fortanase. He is a clinical neurologist in Arcadia, California. The protocol is for caregivers. When families are told their loved ones have cognitive decline, they often want to help but do not know how. We adapted our own way of providing what we felt were critical steps in achieving a workable format. We held the workshop on several occasions. It was interactive, fun and extremely well received.

And, if the stars align just right it is possible that your loved one could improve to the point of returning to you. Don't stop Believing. Some people may call it false hope. We called it faith. With help like this protocol you are a least being given a path to feel You are helping your loved one. Not being told there is nothing you can do.

Legacy's rendition of the famous "Use it or Lose It"

Hippocampus (mind's eye) This is the part of the brain where first symptoms of Alzheimer's begin. The protocol is intended to provoke emotions either positive or negative. It is a very interactive protocol that does not include the use of drugs or supplements. Within the span of your loved one's life you have acquired everything needed for this plan.

You will need to keep a journal daily as a reminder of the steps that were taken each day and the progress achieved. Use this plan as a guide. Experiment with the possibilities. Each person is different and responds in their own way. Good Luck and have fun with this.

Music

Music is such a joyful part of our lives. It enriches our soul. Most of us were even exposed to music of different types in our mother's womb. Music can transcend time and allow us to return to a happy place in our distant past.

Search your memory for music of a song that made an impact on your loved one's life. Sing the song or find a recording. Play it or sing it every day until your loved one can sing along. If perhaps there was music they did not like that can also be used because it stimulates the emotions. A good positive choice would be a wedding song.

Photographs

Remember When? Pictures make time stand still. They are the framework of our lives. Show pictures to your loved one everyday.

It is important to introduce things that happened yesterday or years ago. Just provoke a response, Any response. Even a picture of something or someone they did not like, just get a response. Weddings, Christmas, birthdays, animals, friends, family, the list goes on and on.

We have included some of our favorites for examples. Journal your progress.

Touch

The touch the feel. Amazing what can happen within the body and brain with just one touch. Just one touch and I knew you were for me. Lyrics in a song tell it all. The touch of grass, bark of a tree, a handshake, arms around you for comfort all waken the brain to emotions.

Expose your loved ones to the wonders of nature. Helen Keller is a vivid example of how touch can open up the world to people. Her first realization was the touch of W A T E R. In our day to day life we forget about the wonders. Awaken to the simple things.

Stimulate Smell

The purpose of each step in the TEAM protocol is to provoke emotion or wake up the hippocampus in the brain.

Try to remember aromas that your loved one liked or disliked. Use anything that will trigger a response either negative or positive. Examples: fresh baked cookies, clean clothes, perfume or cologne, fresh cut grass, rose or gardenia. Essential oils can effectively be used because a variety of aromas exist from wild orange to peppermint to cinnamon,etc.

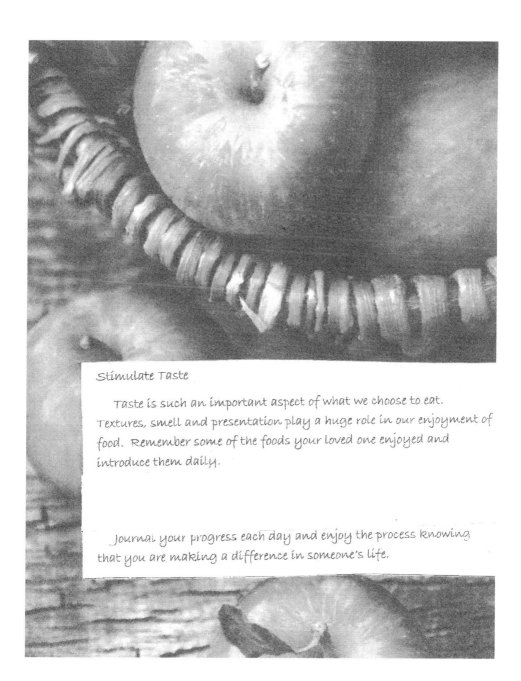

Stimulate Taste

Taste is such an important aspect of what we choose to eat. Textures, smell and presentation play a huge role in our enjoyment of food. Remember some of the foods your loved one enjoyed and introduce them daily.

Journal your progress each day and enjoy the process knowing that you are making a difference in someone's life.

BFF

Research has taught me that being able to continue a lifelong friendship is so beneficial health wise for both people. My BFF and I have been friends over sixty years. She and I do not remember not being friends. Between the two of us our friendship has lasted through four husbands and four children. I call our ability to remain friends through this alone a real accomplishment.

Unconditional love speaks volumes. My BFF and I are so different.

We have chosen to agree to disagree on lots of topics. It allows both of us the ability to be ourselves without feeling judged.

Lifelong friends can give you purpose and if needed a person to be accountable to. Someone that knows your habits and accepts them no matter how different they may seem is very important.

My lifelong friend knew my family and how my adulthood was shaped by my childhood. You can choose to repeat the mistakes of others or you can rise above the situations.

Our friendship has endured also through the deaths of our entire biological families. Many passed away due to long suffering, others lives were cut short by unforeseen tragedy. Grief and loss takes people to uncharted places. You never really know how you or a friend will respond until the unthinkable really happens. Health problems can develop due to various amounts of stress beyond our control.

So, the morning I received a phone call from my friend I knew whatever issue she was dealing with I needed to help. I was aware she had a doctor's appointment the afternoon before. The unsteadiness in her voice let me know the doctor's visit had not gone well. We knew blood sugar issues ran in both of our families. At her appointment, the doctor had given her a prescription and a blood glucose meter. Reality had emerged. After this one bad reading she was immediately placed on medication.

She was quick to let me know, she needed my initial guidance but wanted to be able to control this problem on her own.

At her next appointment her doctor was overwhelmed by her progress. Her doctor told her only two other people during her years of practice had been able to get their blood sugar in check in that length of time.

The doctor also wanted my BFF to accompany her to some of her meetings with diabetic patients. She wanted her to be an example to others that their issue could be positively addressed.

All this reminded me of the many people with this health issue we had helped in our shop and the article that we had written about seeing your reflection in the river. If what you see is not what you want to see shining back then make positive change.

Two important healthcare lessons come from this story:

Keep long time relationships in your life

Understand and tackle your own personal health issues You live in your own life.

You are your own responsibility.

Steve Jobs was right when he said, You can hire someone to run your business for you, drive your car and mow your grass but you cannot hire someone to suffer for you.

Please take the time, the expense and the personal motivation to live as healthy a life as you possibly can.

About the Author

Kathy Hurst R Ph. is a wife, mother and pharmacist of 48 years. She began her healthcare career in hospital and later expanded into clinical, community and retail. But, her passion in pharmacy was always compounding. This passion developed at a young age in her childhood kitchen. Her grandmother was the chef at their restaurant and her grandfather was the herbalist. The memory of the sights and aromas of her childhood lead her to opening her own compounding pharmacy, Legacy Specialty Pharmacy.

Within her business she developed a unique area dedicated to educating people about their health issue and empowering them to think for themselves. She became the bridge between their diagnosis and allowing them to be their own personal advocate. They began to share old and new methods their ancestors had used to heal. This allowed her to engage in a new journey as a pharmacist. One that knows and understands how important old and new methods are to each person's healing.

Now, she spends her retirement time tending vegetables, flowers and herbs at 511 Rains Gardens, her childhood property. She is also co-host at Life in Wellness Podcast and her own podcast A Legacy at 511 Rains.

www.AuthorKathyHurst.com

Made in the USA
Columbia, SC
21 May 2024

a6a71308-133d-40e5-84e4-2788aaa6ba0aR01